Start Writing
About Things
I Do

Penny King
Ruth Thomson

Thameside Press

Distributed in the United States by
Smart Apple Media
1980 Lookout Drive
North Mankato, MN 56003

ISBN 1-930643-51-9

Library of Congress Control Number: 2001088842

Series editors: Mary-Jane Wilkins, Stephanie Turnbull
Designers: Rachel Hamdi, Holly Mann, Angie Allison
Illustrators: Beccy Blake, Kevin McAleenan, Melanie Mansfield,
   Lisa Smith, Sara Walker
Educational consultants: Pie Corbett, Poet and Consultant
   to the English National Literacy Strategy; Sarah Mullen, Literacy Consultant

Printed in Spain

9 8 7 6 5 4 3 2 1

Contents

HOW TO USE THIS BOOK

Can you write a letter, a party invitation, or a menu? This book shows you how.

★

Each double page shows you a different style of writing, such as a menu (shown here). On the left-hand side is an example of the type of writing. On this page it is a menu from a pizza parlor.

Sometimes the writing has labels around it to make it clearer.

★

On the right-hand page are some ideas for creating your own piece of writing. You can choose one of the suggestions or think of something completely different.

A marvelous menu might include these dishes:

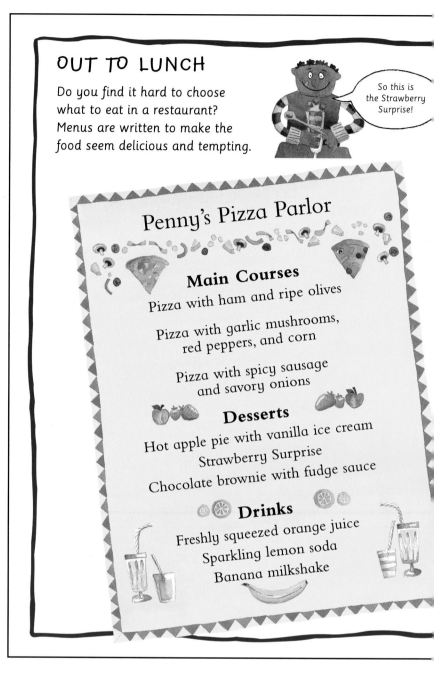

OUT TO LUNCH

Do you find it hard to choose what to eat in a restaurant? Menus are written to make the food seem delicious and tempting.

So this is the Strawberry Surprise!

Penny's Pizza Parlor

Main Courses
Pizza with ham and ripe olives

Pizza with garlic mushrooms, red peppers, and corn

Pizza with spicy sausage and savory onions

Desserts
Hot apple pie with vanilla ice cream
Strawberry Surprise
Chocolate brownie with fudge sauce

Drinks
Freshly squeezed orange juice
Sparkling lemon soda
Banana milkshake

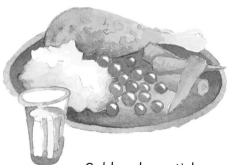

Golden drumsticks with melt-in-the-mouth mashed potato

Tagliatelle covered with tangy tomato sauce

Scrumptious strawberry sponge cake

Now design your own menu.
Use the ideas below to help you.

ain Courses

sserts

RITING TIPS

When you write a menu:

start with the name
of the restaurant.

describe each main course,
dessert and drink.

use a new line for each dish.

decorate the menu with pictures
of the food or the restaurant.

Useful adjectives for food

delicious	scrumptious	yummy
juicy	spicy	creamy
crispy	smooth	hot
icy	sweet	tasty
healthy	wholesome	crunchy

Some pages have a box
of useful words like this:

Useful adjectives for food

delicious	scrumptious	yummy
juicy	spicy	creamy
crispy	smooth	hot
icy	sweet	tasty
healthy	wholesome	crunchy

You can use these to check
your spelling and to make
your writing more interesting.
They are only suggestions!
You will probably think of
other words you could use.

The writing next to the
pencil tells you what
to do. Read this
before you start.

WRITING TIPS

The writing tips remind
you of things you may
need to think about.

CHOOSING A PET

Have you ever wished you could have an unusual pet?

Try making a chart comparing some good and bad things about it before you decide.

I decided that alligators are bad pets because they're not friendly enough.

Alligators are good pets because...	Alligators are bad pets because...
• baby ones are very small. • they don't need exercise. • they can swim in the bathtub. • they are very quiet.	• they grow very big. • they scare the neighbors. • they sometimes eat people. • they are not very cuddly. • they knock things over. • they can be grumpy. • they don't play.

Write some good and bad things
about having a spider or a cat as a pet.

A spider

A cat

WRITING TIPS

Divide your page
into two columns
with a ruled line.

Write this
at the top
of the
left-hand
column.

Write this
at the
top of the
right-hand
column.

Spiders are good pets because...	Spiders are bad pets because...
	• they might scare people. • they are easy to lose. •

Write each
reason on
a new line.

Start each
new reason
with a
bullet point.

Write a final
sentence
that begins
like this
or like this.

I decided that spiders are good pets because...
I decided that spiders are bad pets because...

PARTY TIME

Invitations use only a few words, but they tell you everything you need to know about an event.

The name of the party giver

The name of the guest

The kind of party

The date

The time

The clothes to wear

The person who wants your reply (RSVP is short for the French words "respondez s'il vous plaît" which mean please reply.)

The place

The telephone number or address of the party giver

The King and Queen

invite

the Ugly Sisters

to a ball.

at The Royal Palace
on Saturday April 8
from 8 PM to 1 AM
Dress Ball gowns or uniforms

RSVP The King and Queen **Telephone** 555-3789

The name on the top line

The stamp in the top right-hand corner

The Ugly Sisters
Woodland Cottage
Forest Road
Crownsville, Fairyland

Each part of the address on a separate line

8

Write an invitation for one of these parties.
Decorate it to go with the theme of the party.

A barbecue

A costume birthday party

A princess's christening

WANTED!

How would you catch a big, bad wolf?
One way is to design a WANTED poster like this.

A title in big letter

A pictur of the wanted person

WANTED!
Big, bad wolf wanted for eating granny.

Last seen in the dark woods with little Red Riding Hood, wearing a flowery nightgown and fluffy slippers.

Where the person was last seen

REWARD $500

How much the reward is

If you see the wolf, do not talk to him. Call the police immediately.

A warning

Design a WANTED poster
to catch one of these baddies.
Make it bold and clear.

Goldilocks

WRITING TIPS

When you write your poster:

- put the title—WANTED—at the top.
- describe the baddie and say why he or she is wanted.
- draw a picture of the baddie.
- say where the baddie was last seen.
- say what the reward is.
- tell people what do if they spot the baddie.

Wanted for damaging property.

Hairy Troll

Jack (with his beanstalk)

Wanted for threatening goats.

Wanted for stealing a giant's hen.

READY FOR WORK

What clothes do cooks wear? What equipment do they use?
One way of showing this information is to draw a labeled picture.

EVERYTHING A COOK NEEDS

cutting board

chef's hat

wire whisk

sharp knife

oven mitts

frying pan

colander

apron

dish towel

strainer

grater

scale

mixing bowl

wooden spoon

saucepan

Draw one of these people in their work clothes.
Draw any equipment separately and label everything.
There are some suggestions in the boxes below.

Racing Driver

crash helmet	car	gloves
wheels	hood	tires
seat	wheel	number

Clown

bow tie	big shoes	wig
custard pie	bucket	hoop
false nose	pants	makeup

Doctor

stethoscope	bed	chart
pager	pen	bandage
thermometer	watch	white coat

Monster Hunter

helmet	boots	camera
water bottle	knapsack	hat
binoculars	net	notebook

AROUND TOWN

How would you describe a building?

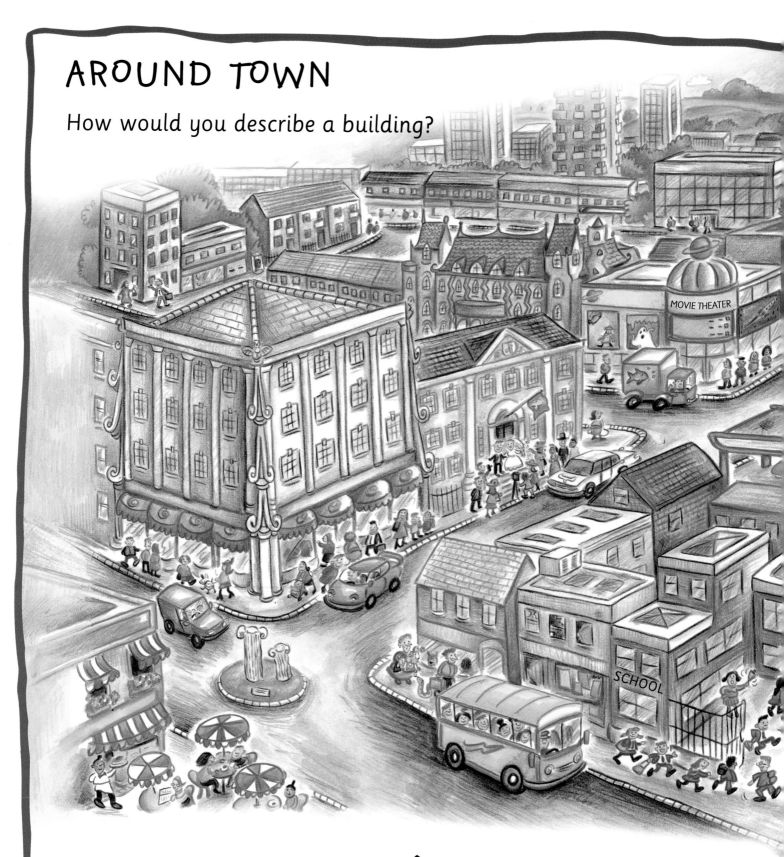

This is a description of a building in the picture above. Which one?

This new building is in the center of town.
It has big posters on the walls outside.
People come here to see films.
It is very busy on Saturday nights.

Choose another building.
Say where it is, what it looks like, and what goes on there. Do not give its name. Ask a friend to guess what it is.

When you describe a building:

- write in the present tense.
- use one or more of these helpful adjectives.

old	ancient	new	modern
tall	small	huge	low
high	square	round	twisted
round	grand	elegant	shabby

- say where the building is.
- point out one of its features. For example, does it have lots of windows or a sign outside?
- say why people go there.
- think of an interesting fact about it.

OUT TO LUNCH

Do you find it hard to choose what to eat in a restaurant? Menus are written to make the food seem delicious and tempting.

So this is the Strawberry Surprise!

Penny's Pizza Parlor

Main Courses

Pizza with ham and ripe olives

Pizza with garlic mushrooms, red peppers, and corn

Pizza with spicy sausage and savory onions

Desserts

Hot apple pie with vanilla ice cream

Strawberry Surprise

Chocolate brownie with fudge sauce

Drinks

Freshly squeezed orange juice

Sparkling lemon soda

Banana milkshake

Now design your own menu.
Use the ideas below to help you.

Menu

Main Courses

Desserts

WRITING TIPS

When you write a menu:

• start with the name
  of the restaurant.

• describe each main course,
  dessert, and drink.

• use a new line for each dish.

• decorate the menu with pictures
  of the food or the restaurant.

Useful adjectives for food

delicious	scrumptious	yummy
juicy	spicy	creamy
crispy	smooth	hot
icy	sweet	tasty
healthy	wholesome	crunchy

SCHOOL RULES

Schools have rules to keep everyone safe and happy.

Ziggle's class made this list of rules for their playground. Which rules are being ignored?

Playground Rules

1. Keep your suckers to yourself.
2. Treat all aliens kindly.
3. Line up sensibly.
4. Leave dangerous pets at home.
5. Put snack wrappers in the trash.
6. Take turns playing on the Twisty Tower.
7. Watch where you are flying.
8. Don't climb on the school walls.
9. Don't fight with lasers.
10. Make sure the playground is empty before you land your space pod.

SCHOOL

What rules would you
make for this playground?

Write a list of ten rules.
Use the picture to help you.
Number each rule and
begin it with a bossy verb.

Bossy verbs

don't	try	put
take turns	watch	line up
go	play	help
share	look	pick up
listen	make sure	ask

MY NEWS

Do you enjoy telling people your news? Billy wrote about his birthday, starting in the morning and ending in the evening.

1.

2.

3.

4.

On Saturday it was my sixth birthday. After breakfast I got my present. It was a racing bike. Then Mom, Dad, Kim, and I went to the park. First I rode my bike. I wobbled a lot! Next we rented a boat. I paddled, but soon I got tired. Later Grandma came for a special meal. My cake was a dinosaur shape. It was my best birthday ever.

This is what Suzy and her brother Matt did on Saturday.
Imagine you are Suzy or Matt and write an account of the day.

1.

2.

3.

4.

 WRITING TIPS

- Begin your account by saying when it happened.

- Say who was with you.

- Tell your reader where you went.

- Say what you did.

- At the end, make a comment about your day.

- Remember to use useful words about time.

first	next	soon
later	afterward	before
finally	then	at last

HIT THE HEADLINES

Does your family read a newspaper?

Imagine if the story of the Queen of Hearts was on the front page. It might look like this.

The Queen of Hearts made some tarts
All on a summer's day.
The Knave of Hearts stole those tarts
and took them clean away.

A short headline

Who the story is about

The name of the writer

What happened

When it happened

Where it happened

The name of the newspaper

A picture of someone in the story

A caption that tells readers about the picture

THE DAILY NEWS

QUEEN'S TARTS STOLEN!

By Ivan Ideer

Police are still hunting for the Knave of Hearts. He is suspected of stealing the Queen's lemon tarts yesterday afternoon. All harbors and airports are being watched in case he tries to leave the country.

The police went to the palace this morning to interview the unhappy Queen, aged 35.

The sad queen in her kitchen.

She said, "I left the tarts by the window to cool. When I came back, they had vanished. I saw the Knave running away in the distance."

The Queen had made the tarts as a surprise for the King's birthday. People from all over the country have sent her hundreds of new tarts.

Retell one of these nursery rhymes as a front-page newspaper story.

Hey, diddle diddle,
The cat and the fiddle,
The cow jumped over the moon.
The little dog laughed to see such sport,
And the dish ran away with the spoon.

Mary had a little lamb,
Its fleece was white as snow.
And everywhere that Mary went,
The lamb was sure to go.
It followed her to school one day
That was against the rule.
It made the children laugh and play
To see a lamb in school.

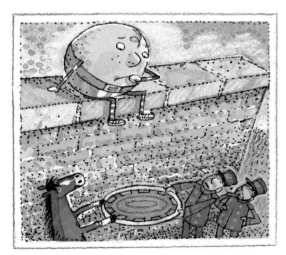

Humpty Dumpty sat on a wall,
Humpty Dumpty had a great fall.
All the King's horses
And all the King's men
Couldn't put Humpty together again.

WRITING TIPS

When you write your newspaper report, make sure you say:

- who it is about.
- what happened.
- when it happened.
- where it happened.
- why it happened (if you know).

GOOD ENOUGH TO EAT

Recipes start with a list of ingredients. They describe how to use the ingredients (the method) and how long it takes to make (the preparation time).

GIANT EGG HERO

Ingredients

- 1 extra-large French bread
- 4 sticks butter (two cups)
- 12 hard-boiled eggs
- 6 tablespoons mayonnaise
- salt and pepper
- 2 heads of lettuce

Method

1. Peel the hard-boiled eggs. Mash them in a bowl with a fork. Add salt and pepper. Stir in the mayonnaise.

2. Cut the French bread in half. Spread butter on both halves.

3. Wash the lettuce and shred.

4. Spread the egg mixture on the bottom half of the bread.

5. Cover it with the shredded lettuce.

6. Finally, put the other half of the bread on top.

Preparation time

15–20 minutes

This recipe is very popular with giants in the summer.

Invent a revolting recipe to delight a dreadful dragon.

Some ideas for ingredients

Useful verbs

add	spread	cut	chop
fill	stir	slice	mix
bake	pour	put	whip
boil	fry	crush	mash

rotten eggs

prickly thistles

moldy bread

wiggly worms

a plump princess

a fat frog

I'm starving. Where's my lunch?

sour grapes

ketchup

WRITING TIPS

When you write a recipe:

- think of a name for it.
- list the ingredients.
- say how much you need of each one.
- describe the method. Make sure you include every ingredient.
- say what must be done first, next, and last.
- number the steps.
- say how long the recipe takes to make.
- at the end, say something interesting about your recipe.

heavy cream

nettle leaves

a string of sausages

fish bones

hot chilies

AMAZING ADS

Advertisements are designed to catch your eye. They try to make you desperate for the thing they advertise.

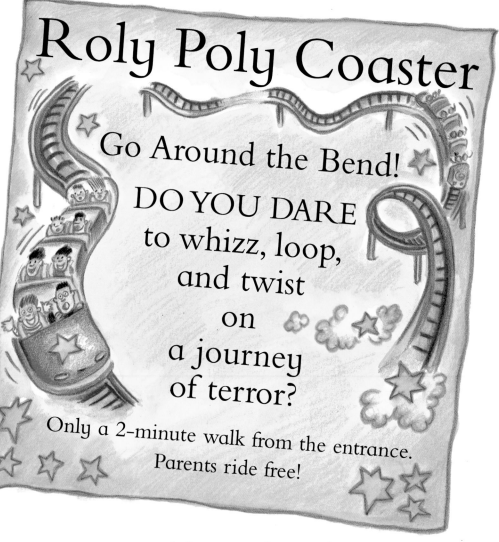

Roly Poly Coaster

Go Around the Bend!

DO YOU DARE
to whizz, loop,
and twist
on
a journey
of terror?

Only a 2-minute walk from the entrance.
Parents ride free!

Write an ad for another ride. Use a few words, clear writing, and bright colors.

Useful verbs

whir	grind	fly	creak
crash	wail	splash	scream
fall	roll	climb	plunge
twist	roar	bounce	spin

When you write your ad:

- think of a short, catchy name for the ride.
- ask questions starting with things like:

    Do you dare...?
    Are you brave enough for...?

- include some verbs to describe what the ride does.
- describe where the ride is.
- remember—people always like something free!

FAN LETTERS

Letters are loads of fun to send and receive.
When you write a letter, remember these things.

Write your address in the top right-hand corner.

Always begin with the word Dear.

Use the person's title and last name.

Ask questions —it is a good way to get an answer!

Write your name and age clearly.

Write today's date under the address.

Say why you are writing.

Look on page 8 to find out how to address an envelope.

25 Castle Drive
Knightsville,
NY 12345

November 3, 2001

Dear Ms. Cox,

I am writing to tell you how much I loved your book, <u>The Dragon's Dinner</u>. I was given it for my birthday.

It was so funny when you wrote about the dragon becoming a vegetarian! We all cried when his mother left him in the zoo because he was so greedy.

Do you use a computer or a pen for writing? It will be Book Week at our school soon, and we wondered if you could come and talk to us about how you write your books. We have lots of questions we would like to ask you.

With best wishes,

Anna Wheeler
(age 7)

Is there someone you really admire?

Surprise them with a fan letter.
Cross your fingers for a reply!

Your favorite sports personality

Your favorite
band or singer

WRITING TIPS

• Put some lined paper under
your writing paper for really
straight lines.

• Here are some different ways
to end your letters:

Yours   Lots of love

Yours sincerely   With best wishes

Love from   Write soon

Your favorite writer

29

LIFE STORIES

The explanation below tells you
how sunflowers grow from seeds.

The Life Story of a Sunflower

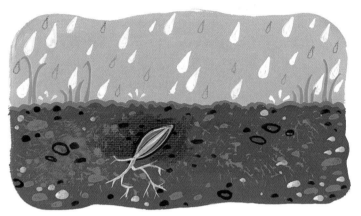

1. The seed swells in warm, wet, spring
weather. The roots push down into the soil.

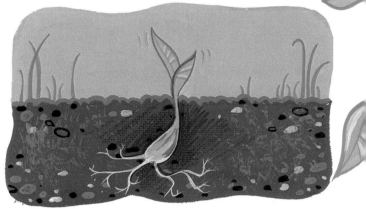

2. A few weeks later, a shoot
appears. The roots keep growing.

3. Next, the leaves start to grow.
The plant grows taller and taller.

4. Soon it is taller than a person.
A flower bud appears.

5. In the summer the bud opens.
The flower turns toward the sun.

6. Later, seeds form, and finally
the petals fade and die.

Use these pictures and labels to tell the life story of a frog. Make sure your explanation is in order.

WRITING TIPS

When you write an explanation:

- first think of a title.
- write in the present tense.
- describe what happens in the right order.
- use time words such as first, then, next, after, and finally.

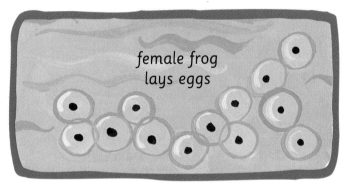

female frog lays eggs

1. Spring.

tadpole hatches

2. After 2 weeks.

breathes through gills

gills

3. After 4 weeks.

back legs grow

gills disappear

breathes air

4. After 8 weeks.

tail shortens

front legs grow

5. After 10 weeks.

becomes froglet

6. After 12 weeks.